BETTER TOGETHER

Unity, Harmony, and Synergy
For the Body of Christ

Dedication

Over the last few years, some of the members of Antioch were called home by the Lord. Their physical remains lay resting in the couch of nature's bosom, awaiting the certain sound of the trumpet in the rapture when our Lord returns. With this in heart, I dedicate this book to each of them and their families. May your hope in Jesus Christ be brought to full fruition when He appears.

This book is further dedicated to five very close and special people in my life who worked on my Staff at the Executive level or volunteered in many capacities throughout our campus. They are gone from my presence but never from my memory. I think of them daily and miss them tremendously:

Sister Malinda Pugh
Culinary Arts Ministry Leader - 26 Years

Sister June Jones
Personal Pastoral Assistant - 26 Years

Deacon Keith "Brou" Broussard
Chairman of Trustees and Executive Director of Plant & Facilities

Deacon Boyd Smith

Honorary Deacon Michael Guillory
Usher President

May they rest eternally in the bosom of God until the redemption of the Rapture becomes our faithful reality.

...to be absent from the body is to be present with the Lord.
2 Cor. 5:8

A 90 - DAY SOJOURN FOR THE FAITHFUL

BETTER TOGETHER

Unity, Harmony, and Synergy
For the Body of Christ

Dr John R. Adolph

Library of Congress Catalog Number: APPLIED FOR	
Name:	Adolph, John R., Author
Title:	*Better Together: A 90-Day Sojourn for the Faithful*
	John R. Adolph
	Advantage Books, 2023
Identifiers:	ISBN Paperback: 978159757498
	ISBN eBook: 978159757610
Subjects:	Books › Religion & Spirituality › Worship & Devotion Devotionals
	Books › Religion & Spirituality › Worship & Devotion Inspirational
	Books › Religion & Spirituality › Worship & Devotion Prayer

First Printing: August 2023
23 24 25 26 27 28   10 9 8 7 6 5 4 3 2 1

Acknowledgments

This work was birthed out of a deep desire to fulfill the Great Commission and the Great Commandment of our Lord Jesus Christ at Antioch Missionary Baptist Church, 3920 West Cardinal Drive in the metropolis of Beaumont, Texas. In this way, when works like this come to fruition, it is never the result of the efforts of just one individual. It requires a collective composite of views, encounters, and skill sets to press it into production. This book is no different.

With this in mind, I must thank my personal Lord and Savior, Jesus Christ, for His death on the cross at Calvary. His love for His bride, the church, and His patience with me as a Pastor. I will be forever indebted to Him as long as I live. May the works that I have done please you my Lord. And may the grace that you have extended to me always speak for me.

To my wife of 27 years, that has been by my side for everything. Through the passing of my mother and father; my failures and successes; through times of great joy and moments of testing and failure. Thank you so much, Lady Dorrie (Baby), for being so steadfast, committed, prayerful, tolerant, loving, caring, faithful, earnest, loyal, and wonderful. May the Lord forever bless you is my sincere supplication. Your growth in Christ as a Disciple maker of women helped to inspire this devotional work. Watching you teach them each Saturday morning made me want to share God's Will and Word with others even more.

To my wonderful children, Sumone and Jonathan, for supporting my work and ministerial sacrifice as a Dad and Pastor. Your growth in God as you matriculate at institutions of academic higher learning has made me so proud of you. I hope this book inspires you to one day pen a work of your own. Remember Philippians 4:13!

To my Executive Director of John R. Adolph Ministries, LLC. Brooklyn D. Williams, who also serves as the Chief of Administration at the church, accepted the daunting task of editing this book by hand and producing this written work not only for Antioch but to be shared with the rest of the world. Thank you for connecting JRA with Advantage Publications. Your diligence, toil, time, and tenacity is not something I could ever pay for, yet I'm extremely appreciative of all you do.

To my Chief Executive Officers of Finance and Ministries, Ms. Felicia Young and Dr. Karen Davis, respectively, and to Rev. Jamison Malbrough, Youth Coordinator for the encouragement to write this devotional for our church family to be used in our Impact Groups. Thank you for reading the manuscript before it was printed and helping me make corrections.

To the full-time staff, part-time staff, and servant leaders of the Lord's Church at Antioch who partner with me in Kingdom building endeavors.

Preface

When people ask me, "How do we make Disciples at Antioch?" my ready response is now simple. We grow Disciples in Jesus Christ through Impact Ministry Groups. With this in mind, our Impact Ministry Groups are simply ministry constructs that exist throughout the church that are present to empower us to fulfill the Great Commission and Great Commandment of our Lord Jesus Christ. Trust me when I say these groups are not just for fellowship. They serve, study, work, and grow disciples; those Disciples make more Disciples. Thus, the Great Commission and Great Commandment live in the church.

In this way, this devotional guide emerged. It grew out of a desire to press our church family closer together in what we sought to give the Lord as it pertains to Christian service. With this in mind, this small devotional guide will serve as our first para source material, designed and developed by me to steer everyone at the church in the same direction.

This book is not a theological treatise on Christian doctrines and dogmas though it contains some of both. This book is simply a ninety-day study guide for the servant members of our congregation to glean, gain and grow from as we seek to work together for the cause of Christ and the glory of our God.

We're Better Together,

Dr. John R. Adolph, Pastor
Antioch Missionary Baptist Church

Dr. John R. Adolph

How To Use This Devotional Book

This small book is a ninety-day journey designed for the members of Antioch Missionary Baptist Church of Beaumont, Texas, to share with each other as we seek to please the Lord through various modes of service and Discipleship. Our Impact Ministries will use this guide each time they gather to grow in God's Word together. We believe that WE ARE BETTER TOGETHER.

Instructions For Antioch Members

Listed below is the template that every Impact Ministry Group should be using. The template is as follows:

IMPACT MINISTRY GROUPS

- During called Ministry meetings add a 15-minute Bible Study
- Take prayer requests and pray for each other
- Intentionally care for the members of your ministry
- Organize, develop, and implement times of faith, fun, and fellowship for the members of your ministry.
- Foster Christian fellowships with a minimum of at least two annually.

Instructions For Non Members

Let me begin by saying thank you for taking this 90-day journey! It is my prayer that it places a sincere desire to know, serve, and share the love of God with others like no other time in your life. With that being said, plan a devotional time with the Lord. Please include a place and time you plan to spend with God each day. Use this like you would a devotional journey.

Instructions For Everyone

The verses at the beginning of each entry are only referenced. With this in mind, please use your Bible and read the entire passage or verse. This will help you hear more of what the Lord says to you daily. After you read the scripture and the journal entry for the day, ask yourself the following devotional questions:

1. How does today's reading affect me?

2. What do I feel led to do after reading today's lesson?

3. What more could I do for the Lord based on what I read?

Day 1
"…..we have fellowship with one another…." 1 John 1:7

SOME THINGS ARE JUST BETTER TOGETHER

You can eat cereal by itself, but it's better with milk. You can eat jelly by itself, but it is better on a nice brown piece of toast. You can eat salt by itself, but it has more purpose if you sprinkle it on food that can use a slight boost. You can eat rice by itself, but there's something about a good gravy that makes it taste so much better. You can brush your teeth with just a toothbrush, but toothpaste can help you fix the real problem, morning breath. Here's the point of our initial lesson, some things are just better together. When John writes the phrase "….we have fellowship with one another…." he uses the word Koinonia to describe how Christians should relate to each other. The term means to speak the same language. It suggests that language unites us for a common cause so that we are never alone. For the believer who is a Christian, WE LOVE JESUS CHRIST! And, our love for Him makes us fit for each other. In this vein, we gain strength from each other; we gain wisdom from each other, and we are blessed by one another. Never forget this, Christians can walk by faith alone. However, it would be like eating cereal without milk or using a toothbrush without toothpaste. Just like those things are better together, so are we.

Day 2
"Bear ye one another's burdens…." Gal. 6:2

LET ME HELP YOU WITH THAT

Have you ever heard these words before? They can be like music to your ears when you are carrying a heavy load. They spell relief when what you are trying to carry is too much for you to bear. Students from Lamar University were moving back on campus for the start of a new semester. Some students had boxes, bags, crates, and baskets filled with a little bit of everything. The Texas sun was hot, and loads were heavy. A young lady was trying to carry a huge box up a flight of stairs when a young man wearing a t-shirt that said "Fellowship of Christian Athletes" said, "Let me help you with that!" A huge sigh of relief appeared on the brow of that young lady. Why? Someone was there to help her handle her heavy load. Here's a great devotional question to grapple with as we share this devotional moment today, "What's heavy on your heart right now?" The good news is this; you do not have to deal with burdens alone. It is why Paul teaches the churches of Galatia that we, as Christians, have to be in a mode of helping each other deal with life's heavy burdens. Keep this in mind. We help each other for two reasons. First of all, we were told to do it. And secondly, because you never know when your burden will be too heavy for you, and you'll need to hear the words that bring relief to your soul from a fellow believer in Jesus Christ that say, "Let me help you with that." Burdens are always lighter when shared by someone who helps you handle them.

Day 3
"Wherefore comfort yourselves together…and edify one another…." 1 Thess 5:11

ALL I NEEDED WAS A LITTLE PUSH

Central Park is a beautiful recreational playground in the metropolis of Beaumont, Texas that is filled with old school outdoor activities: monkey bars, a jungle jim, merry-go-round and swings. One day a little girl was on a swing with her friend and she was having a really hard time getting started. Her friend however was soaring and swinging and having a good time. All of a sudden the kindest gesture took place ever. The kid that was soaring stopped her swing, got behind her friend and gave her a little push. And from that push, her buddy soared too! That is the modern day picture of what Paul writes to the church in Thessalonica when he exhorts us to "…edify one another…" It means to simply encourage one another. In a practical sense, it means that every now and then all we really need is a little push. Have you been there before? Have you ever needed a whisper of encouragement or even just a smile from a friend that says "keep your head up?" It happens to all of us from time to time. In fact, this is something you can do today for a brother or sister in Christ. Give someone just a little push. It could change the outcome of their day and the trajectory of their tomorrow.

Day 4
".....the members should have the same care one for another." 1 Cor. 12:25

I WAS JUST CHECKING ON YOU

There are times when even the strongest Christians feel weak and worn. Truthfully, it is just a part of the typography of the Christian sojourn on Earth. During those moments, we can be extremely vulnerable to thoughts of defeat, despair, and even moments of depression. Have you ever been there before? It's during those times we need each other the most. Lanis Myles had suffered the sudden loss of her husband, and of course, it took a severe toll on her in every way imaginable, including attending church regularly. One Friday evening, the Lord pushed a friend from her choral group to call her. When Lanis' phone rang, she was hesitant to answer because she did not recognize the number on her caller id display. But, thank God she did. When Lanis said "hello," her friend from the choir said, "Lanis, I was just checking on you," and the tears began to flow. When Paul says that members should "care for one another," his word choice is Merimosi. This term comes from Greek medicine. It is a picture of a doctor checking on a patient. It simply means to look after someone with genuine concern for their well-being. Just like that one phone call helped Lanis Myles, your concern for someone other than yourself will bless them. So what are you waiting on? Get busy. Make the call, and when they answer, simply say, "I was just checking on you."

Day 5
".....and forgiving one another….." Col. 3:13

I DECIDED TO BLESS MYSELF

All blessings come from the Lord. God blesses what He wants to bless; He does what He wants to do, and no one can do anything about His decisions. After all, the Lord is God; besides Him, there is none other. But what if there was a way for you to bless yourself? Would you do it? Here's how it's done, and always remember it. Forgive those that have hurt you. In most instances, people find forgiveness hard to do. This is because we often see forgiveness as letting people get away with a horrible deed when revenge would seem much better. However, here's something to think about. True forgiveness is a very selfish act. Forgiveness is best defined as when you decide to release the prisoner from the pain and hurt that others have caused, only to realize that you are the prisoner wearing handcuffs. If you are reading this devotional, it is not by accident. And, if you are reading this article, it is by divine providence. Consider this a personal note from God giving you full permission to bless yourself. Release the pain, the hurt, the bitterness, the damage, and the deeds caused by others that have left you scared and move on. When all is finished, you will bless yourself.

Day 6
".....forbearing one another in love;" Eph. 4:2c

JUST BE PATIENT WITH ME

It's been said that "patience is a virtue". The only problem with this philosophy is that many of us cannot wait long enough to see if it's true. Let's get straight to the point here; the word "wait" is equivalent to modern-day profanity. We don't like waiting on anything or anybody. We don't want to wait in line. We don't want to wait for a table at a restaurant. And we do not want to wait for true maturity to take place. As Paul writes to the church at Ephesus, he presses them to "forbear one another in love." This phrase is so rich. It means to watch a fig tree bear fruit. Hey, did you know that a fig tree can take up to three years before it can produce sweet figs good for human consumption? The moral of the story here is simple. If you want some figs, you must "forbear" a fig tree long enough to see it bear fruit. In short, it will require patience. The kitchen looked like a hazmat zone on a construction site. Why do you ask? Because this newly wedded wife could not cook. She served her hubby scrambled eggs filled with eggshells, toast that was burnt, and grits that had been scorched. She served his plate and looked at him with a smile on her face, and said, "Just be patient with me. After all, good things come to those that wait." And so it is with us. Tell people who are exposed to your flaws "just be patient with me …..good things come to those who wait."

Day 7
"And be ye kind one to another….." Eph. 4:32a

IT'S JUST GOOD TO BE GOOD

It's nice to be nice. It's kind to be kind. And it's just good to be good. Have you ever heard any of these little epitaphs before? If you are like most, you have. The reason for this is that they make good sense. Phrases like these flowed from the hearts of our matriarchs and patriarchs that taught us the faith of the Lord Jesus Christ well. With this in mind, reading and obeying the Bible can be challenging. Verses like this can be tough for mean Christians who can be anything but "kind." Quick question for you to consider. Have you ever met a mean Christian with a Bible under their arm sitting on a pew in church? Wait, let's press the matter a little further. Have you ever been mean to someone, and you knew it? Remember this. We are told to be kind because it reminds others who encounter us of the King we seek to serve. Just like the Bible says, "Do not steal," it also says, "...be ye kind one to another." Let's give today's lesson some legs, shall we? Find someone to practice on and express a random act of kindness towards them. It's just good to be good, and practice makes perfect!

Day 8
"Finally,....having compassion one of another...." 1 Pet. 3:8a

CAN'T WE ALL JUST GET ALONG

"Can't we all just get along?" This query has been settled into the social consciousness of America since the mid-1980s. It was an incident that we should never forget that took place in the City of Angels. Rodney King was mauled by LA police officers while being recorded on VHS tape, and the officers who beat him were later found not guilty. The event led to social upheaval like only that era could record it. Yet, in response to the racial madness that was taking place from border to border and from sea to sea, Rodney King in an interview with scars still on his face from the beating that he had taken, simply said, "Can't we all just get along?" Compassion is best defined as you feeling what hurts someone else. In short, you stand in my shoes, and I'll stand in yours so I can feel what you feel and vice-versa. With this in mind, Peter contends that the root of compassion produces the sweet fruit of unity. If you want to see a church grow, a ministry gain strength, and a family really come together, stop looking at life only through your lenses and look at life through the lenses of others. Can't we all just get along? Yes, if we have compassion for one another.

Day 9
"....in honour preferring one another." Romans 12:10c

R-E-S-P-E-C-T

Aretha Franklin rocked the whole nation when she released her hit in the early 1970s. People were singing it, shouting it, and dancing to it worldwide. You can hear the melody in your heart if you listen carefully right now. Can you hear it? "RESPECT find out what it means to me. Take care of TCB! Sock it to me, sock it to me!" In a very practical sense, the term respect is the true meaning of the word "honor" that Paul uses when he writes the church in Rome to discuss and define how we treat each other. Paul is not saying bow to them. What he is teaching is that we should have mutual respect. This is crucial to how we relate to one another because we all see life differently. But remember this, different does not have to be wrong; it just means it is different. You like your grits with cheese, and I eat my grits with sugar. Don't try to change me; I won't try to change you. What we will do is respect each other's views and learn to embrace our differences and share our similarities. It's what the Bible calls honor and how we practice RESPECT.

Day 10
"....and forgiving one another, if any man have a quarrel against any: even as Christ forgave you, so also do ye." Col. 3:13

I'M GONNA LET YOU MAKE IT

Something strange happened at a house blessing once. A young lady, a single parent of three, placed a picture of her verbally and physically abusive ex on her coffee table. When people asked who he was, she would proudly respond, "he's my ex-husband." Strange right? But here's the deal, it wasn't until she forgave him that her life made a complete turnaround for the better. When she released him, God released blessings like never before! She graduated from college with a degree in nursing as an RN, received a job that hired her with a $10,000 signing bonus and used the bonus to help her get her new house. This young lady told everyone that nothing changed for the better until she called her ex-husband and said, "I'm gonna let you make it." Here's a devotional question: "Is unforgiveness blocking any of your blessings today?" Here's another good question: "Have you ever been hurt by church folk you haven't forgiven yet?" If so, here's some sound Biblical advice, bless yourself and "Let Them Make It!"

Day 11
"....speaking to one another...." Eph. 4:15

SPEAK WHEN YOU WALK INTO THE ROOM

If you grew up "old school," you have heard these words before. People raised by folk from 1980 and before had different morals, values, and social etiquette than most of us today. For example, they believed that if you dropped it, you should pick it up. If you make a mess, you should clean it up; if you walk into a room; you should speak to the people present. When Paul instructs the Ephesian Christians to "...speak to one another...." this is what he has in mind. He is saying that your speaking to others is connected to how you feel about the Almighty. With this in mind, you should always make speaking to others in a Christian environment a common practice because we are all family in the faith. Take a moment and consider this thought, "if everyone at my church were just like me, what kind of church would my church be?" Do you speak to people when you are in a worship setting? Do you say hello at home? Here's the bottom line, you should practice speaking starting today if you don't. And remember, you're speaking to them because you want them to know about the God who lives in you.

Day 12
"....submit one to another in the fear of God...." Eph. 5:21

MY MARRIAGE WAS A MESS UNTIL....

Okay, here's the truth, the whole "happily ever after" thing doesn't happen until you've gone through quite a bit. In most cases, men run into trouble trying to get their wives to submit to them because of gender-related notions. They soon find out that gender definition alone will not get the job done. When Paul tells the Ephesian church how to behave in marriage, he begins with mutual submission first. This means that the man and the woman both submit to God. The term "submit" is hupataso in Greek. It sounds like "hot potato" in English because that's what you'll get if you try to make a woman submit to you just because you're a man. Here's the blessing of it all, mutual submission to God means mutual respect, love, trust, and faith. Wallace Wilson's marriage was a mess until he learned this lesson with his wife of now over fifty years. Within the first few years, he was headed for divorce and disaster alley. But, he discovered that bowing his knee to God in total submission compelled his wife to submit to him humbly. It is a beautiful portrait of how marriage can genuinely work!

Day 13
"....wherefore comfort one another with these words...." 1 Thess. 4:18

YOU'RE GONNA MAKE IT THROUGH THIS

Life can hurt, and when it does, you will need some novocaine for the pain. You will need something to help you with the hurt you are trying to endure. It does not matter whether it is the loss of a job, the death of a loved one, the diagnosis of an illness, a financial atrocity, or a relationship that is beyond fractured and is now actually shattered. You will need something to get you through that moment. Have you ever been there before? Paul tells the church in Thessalonica to "comfort one another with these words." In short, he says when you can see a saint going through a tough time, your words can bring them ease and comfort. Sonya's mother had passed away, and it was a real struggle for her. While standing in worship one Sunday morning, a mother of the church passed by and could see her struggle on her brow, took her by the hand, and said, "You're gonna make it through this," and she's been making it ever since. Perhaps your hurt is real today. Consider this devotional a love note from God that says, "You're gonna make it through this"!

Day 14
"Be of the same mind toward one another...." Rom. 12:16

WHAT'S YOUR SIGN?

In the mid-1970s, galaxy gazers had everyone looking to the stars for proof of relational compatibility. Pisces is compatible with Leo but not with Gemini, and the list goes on. But you do not need stars to tell you who you are compatible with. You only need a word from the Son. In God's Word, Paul writes to the church in Rome and says to them, "Be of the same mind toward one another." A better translation of this pericope would be to say, live in harmony with one another. Harmony is so beautiful. It is a musical term that connotes and suggests that notes on a scale can be different, but, when used together can be wonderful. In short, harmony happens when you discover that E flat, B flat, F sharp, and A natural are different keys. But if you skillfully play them together, they can make beautiful music. Today's core of this lesson: God loves variety and made us all very different. No matter what your sign is, we can live in harmony with one another when we embrace the fact that we are different and celebrate what we have in common. "What's your sign?" used to be the question of the day. But a better question for us today might be, "Who's your Daddy?" When God is your Father, all His Children have the capacity to get along in sweet harmony.

Day 15
"Exhort one another daily...." Heb. 3:13a

LOCKER ROOM TRASH TALK

There's nothing like it in the world. Before a team goes to battle, they huddle in the locker room for trash talk. It is where they exhort one another before the battle begins. It happens when they come together knowing that the competition is ahead of them, but they celebrate victory before the contest begins. In a practical sense, this is precisely what the writer of Hebrews instructs Christians to do with one another every day. My friends, when we rise to the grace of a new day, we have no idea what challenges we will face, what demons will attack our families, and what satanic setbacks we will suffer. But the good news is that we have each other to lean on and find encouragement from. Chances are you are not in a locker room at the moment. But that does not mean you can't find someone to encourage in the faith. Take a moment and send a word of exhortation to three friends on your mobile device. Your words may cause them to win!

Day 16
"Confess your faults one to another....." James 5:16a

GOOD FOR THE SOUL, BAD FOR THE REPUTATION

Okay, so let's clear the air right away. Confession can be healing, therapeutic, and a blessing in many ways. Sharing your issues with someone can be like letting air out of a balloon just about to burst. However, please understand this; you cannot confess your faults to everyone. In short, some people need help to handle your areas of struggle. And others cannot deal with you being flawed because, from where they stand, you appear to be perfect. To discover that you are not could be damaging to them. So with great discretion, take these words of wisdom to heart, "confess your faults one to another." When James admonishes Christians who are scattered abroad to "confess their faults one to another," he is saying to them is find security by sharing with other Christians areas of growth for them, especially in areas where they need God's strength. Here's an excellent devotional question to ponder today. What is a real area of growth for you? What is one area that causes you to confront your greatest shortcomings? Remember this: confession can be good for the soul but bad for the reputation. Confess your areas of growth and struggle with Christians who can discuss their struggles with you. If they can't talk about theirs, chances are they will talk about yours, just not with you. Be wise!

Day 17
"….and pray for one another that ye may be healed….." James 5:16b

COVER ME!

The Westerns of old were some great movies to watch. In every Western, there would be a scene where the Cowboys would be trapped under heavy fire from the dangerous arrows of the Indians. The only hope for the Cowboys would be for one of them to escape to safety to call in the cavalry. Then, you would hear these words, "Cover me!" That was a way of saying shoot as much as you can against the enemy for me, and if I make it, I promise to find a way to turn around and help you. My friend, when believers pray for one another, this is what happens. When James encourages believers to pray for one another, it is so that we might discover two things. One, God does answer our prayers. And two, when we pray for others, we bless ourselves. The passage says, "….that ye may be healed." When we cover others, the Lord covers us. No good Western ends without a hopeless scene. It's the moment when the enemy is closing in, and the Cowboys have no more bullets to fire. And, all of a sudden, the one that had been covered returns with the calvary! Thank God for those that we cover in prayer! To help them is to heal you.

Day 18
"….Yea, all of you be subject one to another….." 1 Pet. 5:5

BRING IT DOWN A NOTCH!

If pride comes before the fall, humility comes before you rise. The Bible often teaches in paradoxes. A paradox is the truth standing upside down on its head, yelling to get your attention. For example, if you want to be in first place, you fight to get to the front of the line. But the Christian paradox says just the opposite. The Bible says, "…the last shall be first, and the first shall be last." The world says fighting is the only way to get to the top. But, the believer's paradox says if you want to get to the top, bring it down a notch. You see when you crawl to the bottom, God will then elevate you to the top. When Peter says, "…be subject one to another…" he is saying to work in the spirit of Christ to keep each other humble. Remind yourself and others that without God, we have nothing, and it is because of Him that we have everything. Remind yourself and others that every good and perfect thing in your life is due to His kindness, blessing, and favor. And when a spirit of pride creeps into your mind and starts to make you think that you did it all by yourself, remember the words of Peter and the title of this little devotional lesson…."Bring it down a notch."

Day 19
"....consider another to provoke unto love and good works...." Heb. 10:24

STIR IT UP!

The word "provoke" used in this passage comes from a Greek term that means to "stir." It was used in the Greek culinary sense to mix the eggs from a chicken to make other things like unleavened bread, sweet loaves, and even cakes. Speaking of cakes, there is nothing like watching a real culinary master bake a cake. Why? Because they have to take that batter and stir it up. You see, stirring it up helps to get all of the ingredients in the bowl to come together. In this sense, the Bible puts ".....love and good works...." together in a bowl because to have one without the other is a waste of time. Love without works is only a good idea. Works without love is nothing more than an activity without accomplishment. Love and works produce a culinary masterpiece called Christianity. Just imagine what it would have been like to hear Jesus Christ say, "I love you," and never die on the cross as proof of His commitment. Today heaven is shouting to the believers on Earth to stir it up! Propel and compel one another to love and do good work! When the church is at its strongest, we are prayerfully loving, encouraging, and exhorting each other to serve the Lord by serving others in the Kingdom of our God.

Day 20
"....teaching and admonishing one another....." Col. 3:16

HOOK ME UP!

There used to be an automobile commercial highlighting the importance of seat belts. The commercial showed an artificial person riding in a car, crashing into a brick wall. The commercial said, "You can learn a lot from a dummy." Are you old enough to remember that? If we can learn a lot from a dummy, we should be able to learn even more from each other. Paul writes the Colossians and tells them they should be "teaching and admonishing one another." In this vein, a better translation would be to suggest that we should be learning and growing from one another. Not long ago, a young man from our church wanted to plant a garden in his backyard. But, he thought that collard greens came from the grocery store. That's a nice way of saying he had no clue about gardening or growing anything. But, he discovered that an older Deacon of the church had greens and okra growing in his yard like crazy. That young man called that old Deacon and said, "I heard through the grapevine you had greens growing in your yard. Will you please hook me up?" That phone call grew a wonderful relationship where the old taught the young how to make it happen in the field. When you see a saint praying, and you don't know how to pray, tell them to hook you up. When you see a strong Christian learn the Bible, but you don't know how to study yours, tell them to hook you up! It's true. You can learn a lot from a dummy. But, we can learn even more from one another. If you find someone with wisdom and knowledge, say, "Hook me up!"

Day 21
"….let each esteem other better than themselves…."   Phil. 2:3

WE COULDN'T WIN THIS THING WITHOUT YOU!

The Beaumont United Timberwolves were in the State Boy's basketball Championship in 2022. They were pitted against a tough Dallas team that was giving them a fit in every direction. The kids from Dallas would not die. Senior power forward Terrance Arceneaux, took the final shot, which proved to be a buzzer-beater that caused the Timberwolves to win the State Boys Basketball Championship by just one point. When the game was over, Arceneaux said to one of his teammates that didn't get any playing time during the game, something the church could learn great lessons from. He simply told him, "We couldn't win this thing without you!" There are times when God graces us with His favor. And, as Christians, we can use it to make people feel small or cause them to feel valued and important. Paul puts the lesson like this "…let each esteem other better than themselves." It is a good way of saying to others what Arceneaux said to his teammate "We couldn't win this thing without you!" Here's a good question to ponder. When was the last time you used your influence to make someone feel included and important? Have you ever worked to make someone who contributed less know that every contribution is important, including theirs? That's what Christian teamwork is all about. It is about ensuring that everyone feels like a contributor, no matter how small or large.

Day 22
"….but every man also on the things of others…." Phil. 2:4

IT'S NOT JUST ABOUT YOU!

This may seem like a complete shocker to you, but it's true nonetheless, life is not just about you! Of course, we live in an era of narcissists that think that everything is about them. It is the "selfie" generation that thinks that nothing can happen without them. But here's the truth: you are a key part of everything that happens around you, but it is not about you. It is really about God and what He is doing with all of us that is most important. Here's what the Bible says about this: Paul wrote to the Philippian Church and said, "…..but every man also on the things of others…." A better translation of this verse would be written like this, "…..everybody counts in the family of God, so it's not just about what you have done." The game show Jeopardy has been a hit for years. Contestants win big prizes when they spell words with missing letters correctly. When Christians in the body of Christ want to become great, they drop the "U," pick up the "H" and the "M," and buy the vowel "I." Together it spells the one word that reminds all of us that it is not about you. It is all about HIM! Serve HIM! Worship HIM! Praise HIM! Bless HIM! Honor HIM! Share HIM with our friends and family! It is not just about you. It's all about HIM!

Day 23
"....love one another...." John 13:34

IT'S A COMMAND, NOT A SUGGESTION!

Our nation's military is one of the strongest in the known world. The root of its strength is seen in the fact that soldiers know how to follow commands. You see, commands are not suggestions. To be granted suggestions means that you have options and choices. But when a set of commands are given, they must be followed. Like a commander in the Army, our Lord of Hosts does not give suggestions. He gives commands. One of the greatest commands that He has ever given is found in our lesson today. John writes it on this wise, "....love one another...." There are no if's, and's, or but's about it. This command is not designed to suit how you feel about a particular person. It is not given based on whether or not you are in the mood to love the individual or not. It is given based on the fact that God has commanded it, and that command is not a suggestion at all. Two little boys got into a brawl in the Dollar Store over a rubber ball that was being purchased at the counter for them to play with. The young mother of the boys broke them up and made them hug in front of everybody. They did not want to do it. It was then this mother used her maternal authority. She said loudly, "I said hug! It's a command, not a suggestion!" Friends, our Lord shouts the same command at us each day. "....love one another..." It's a command, not a suggestion!

Day 24
"....love one another...." John 13:35

THE TRUE TRADEMARK

You have to watch what you purchase from Amazon. You see, everything that looks real isn't. Some of the merchandise can be considered a knock off items. They are not real. They look real, but they are just not authentic. When an item is real, it bears an insignia called a trademark. It is a seal of approval from the manufacturer that says, "This item is the real deal." As a believer in Jesus Christ, God is our creator manufacturer, and like any great maker, He seals His product with His trademark. The problem today is that churches can be filled with "knock-off Christians" that appear real, but are fake. What determines if a Christian is real or not? It is not how many spiritual gifts they have. It is not how much money they might put into the church. It's not even how many ministries they serve in. The trademark of a Christian is simply this. They know how to ".....love one another...." Jesus said, "By this shall all men know that you are my disciples." In short, being a hateful Christian makes a person not be a Christian. Being a loveless believer in Jesus means you have not met Jesus at all. Love. It is what makes God who God is, and it is what makes a real Christian real. It's the trademark!

Day 25
"....love one another...." John 15:12

AND THERE'S NOTHING YOU CAN DO ABOUT IT!

The show "Undercover Boss" is now in its 5th season. It's doing so well because it demands your attention and makes you watch if you're a little nosy and can stomach the suspense. Not long ago, on the show, the CEO of one of the nation's largest companies called an employee to award her an increase in compensation for doing a good job. But after listening to her voicemail, he changed his mind and decided to promote her to the company's Vice President of Diversity, Equity, and Inclusion. Her voicemail said, "I can't take your call right now because I'm busy helping to build one of the greatest companies in the world. However, I promise to call you back when time permits. And remember this, I love you, and there's nothing you can do about it."

The CEO hung up the phone and enthusiastically exclaimed, "Promote her today!" You see, her saying pleased the CEO. Did you know Christians have an "undercover boss," too? He takes great joy when those that work for His company love people like He does. Take a moment and read St. John 15:12 and make up your mind to love people to the point that your love for them has nothing to do with them, but it's a decision you made. One that says, "And there's nothing you can do about it!"

Day 26
"....love one another...." John 15:17

WHO MASHED THE REPEAT BUTTON?

So if you're reading this devotional study by now, you must ask yourself, "Who mashed the repeat button?" For the last few days, we have been studying different verses in the Bible that are all saying the same thing. It is like a loud echo in the canyon that keeps saying, ".....love one another...." It's not that anyone has mashed the repeat button; however, ".....love one another....." is the most repeated command in the entire Bible. The certainty of its repetition rests in the fact that it is just that important. God keeps repeating it because He does not want you to miss it, and He does not want you to disobey it. So for the sake of redundancy and repetition, read it, remember it and recall it when necessary. The most repeated command in the entire Bible is simply this, "love one another....love one another....love one another....love one another.....love one another.....love one another....love one another.....love one another....love one another.....love one another.....love one another!"

Day 27

"….love one another…." 1 John 3:11

BUT GOD, THEY GET ON MY LAST NERVE!

Okay, let's be brutally honest today. Some people are not easy to love. Some people are evil, messy, ungrateful, hypocritical, abusive, narrow-minded, judgemental, and satanically induced with a spirit you cannot stand. Let's be human for a moment and deal with the fact that there are just some people you don't like. And, while we are at it, let's add that some people you don't care for get on your last nerve. How can we possibly love people like this? We love them by coming to grips with two faithful facts that we, as Christians, are challenged to live by. First of all, God has allowed the people that you cannot stand to be present in your life. They are there by divine design. And, what the Lord wants you to do is make a decision to love them just like He has made a decision to love you. Secondly, they are present so that God can show people what it is like to know Him, and He will use you to do it so you can't afford to mess it up. The bottom line is that they get on your nerves, but it's not about your nerves. It is really about God's needs. God needs you to love them so He can use you to show the world what it is like to know Jesus Christ!

Day 28

"….love one another…." 1 John 3:23

AND DON'T YOU FORGET IT

There is a school for dogs in Beaumont, Texas, called United K-9 Academy. Not long ago, they displayed a crew of dogs on social media to advertise how they train dogs for service. The most amazing thing about the training program was the fact that the Master Trainer repeated the same commands over and over and over again. It was like he was stuck on repeat times 10! When the show ended, the host asked the trainer why they repeated the commands so much. And his response was amazing. The trainer said, "the more you repeat a command, the more the animal learns to love and trust you." He said to repeat commands is not just about obedience and memory. It's about love and trust. If this is true, it could be why this command is the most repeated in the entire Bible. God wants us to love and trust Him like never before. In 1 John 3:23, we are reminded by God not to forget this commandment. This command has been repeated thirteen times at this point in the canon. So this is not just about redundancy and clarity but also God's need and necessity. God said "…..love one another…." And don't you forget it!

Day 29
"....love one another...." 1 John 4:7

WHAT IS GOD REALLY LIKE?

Vacation Bible School was in full swing. The theme for the week was "Getting To Know God!" In one of the kids' classes, the teacher did an exercise where she asked the students to take out a sheet of paper and draw what they thought God was really like. One kid drew a beautiful forest filled with trees. Another kid drew an ocean filled with fish. But one kid drew a picture of himself. When the VBS teacher asked the little boy who was on his paper, he said with great pride, "Don't be silly. It is me. I drew myself." The teacher asked why on Earth would you do that? The little boy said, "You said God was love, and I love everybody, so God is just like me!" What a discovery! God is like me because love is God, and God is love. When John writes the phrase ".....love one another....." he is categorically saying since God is love, the believer that loves is just like God. This is why love is so powerful. We are most like animals when we seek revenge. We are most like our adversary when we learn to hate. But we are most like God when we learn to love. God is really like love!

Day 30
"....love one another...." 1 John 4:11

JUST DO IT

Nike is the greatest sports equipment manufacturer in the known world. Addidas, Puma, and Under Armor may not agree, but it's true. With this in mind, Nike has adopted a mantra that should live in the hearts of every believer in Jesus Christ when it relates to love and how we treat one another. Here's what Nike says, "JUST DO IT!" Friends, loving one another is more than a notion. It is a statement of faith and our true thoughts of how we feel about Jesus Christ. To say that we love God but hate our fellow man puts us in great danger with God. The Apostle John puts the same argument this way, "After all, how can you say that you love God, who you have never laid an eye on and cannot muster up enough faith to love people that you see every day" (MSG. Bible, Peterson)? The real truth is that if you cannot love others, you may not love God at all. This is tough teaching, but it is the root of Christianity. The Great Commandment of the Lord Jesus Christ states that we should "...love our neighbor as we love ourselves..." (Matt. 22:34-40, focus vs. 39). So when it comes to this command given in scripture, the only way to make it live is for you to make up your mind to DO IT! Put your feelings aside, pick up your faith, and JUST DO IT! Forgive the things they have done and their spoken words, and JUST DO IT! Make this commandment of the Lord live by saying to yourself when it comes to loving others, I will not compromise; I will JUST DO IT!

Day 31
"….love one another...." 1 John 4:12

NO EXCUSES

There's a poetic refrain that says, "Excuses are tools of the incompetent. They build monuments of nothingness. Those who choose to use them seldom amount to anything." Though this statement is not Biblical, it is practical and usable when it comes to having a good reason not to love others. Remember, to love one another is not some warm fuzzy feeling. It is not you forgetting what was said, removing what was done from your mind, or acting as if it never happened. To love one another means that you have made a clear, conscious, Christ-centered decision to extend to others what the Lord has extended to you. To love one another is an affirmation of faith that says though I am not God, I love God enough to show you what God is like. Churches are empty, families are wounded, people are scared, and relationships struggle on every level because we lack obeying this one repetitious command. To love one another is not an act of stupidity; it is an expression of humility. To love one another is not a display of weakness; it is the discipline of Christian meekness. To love one another is not about your feelings; it is, however, an indicator that shows you how you feel about God. Here's the command again, "love one another." No excuses.

Day 32
"O how good and pleasant it is for brethren to dwell together in Unity."   Psalms 133:1

THIS IS AS GOOD AS IT GETS

The family reunion was at an all-time high. The ribs were smoking, the dominoes were slamming, the kids were playing, and the ladies were laughing and gossiping. It was time to dine, and everyone gathered in a circle to bless the food. Dr. A. G. Robinson said, "Look at what the Lord has done for us today. We are all here! Loving each other, having a good time, and we are together. In my soul, this is as good as it gets!" Reading Psalms 133 gives the feel and function of a faith that makes people feel a sense of family unity. Please remember that there is a difference between harmony, synergy, and unity. Harmony suggests that we are different, but when we work together towards a common goal, our differences make us complete. Synergy takes place when we mix what is negative with positive things to create something that moves everything forward. But unity happens when we take harmony and synergy and plait them together. Unity is extremely powerful. A united team fights together for victory. A united company strives for the common goal of making things profitable. And a united church that honors Christ is undefeated with God on its side. Division is a Kingdom killer. Unity is a Kingdom builder. When believers in the Lord Jesus Christ stand together in unity, we can echo the sentiment of Dr. A. G. Robinson and say, "This is as good as it gets!"

Day 33
"Two are better than one….." Eccl. 4:9

WHEN WE'RE TOGETHER, THINGS GET BETTER

When hurricanes hit the Gulf Coast, people run for cover. Pastor Aldon Cotton of New Orleans helped his entire church family evacuate together when Hurricane Ike came ashore in 2008. He quickly noticed that as long as they were together, things just got better, but they struggled to make it when they were apart. You will need believers to help you make it when life hits rough spots. The writer of Ecclesiastes put it like this, "Two are better than one because they have a good reward for their labor." What the writer is saying is that when we work together as one cohesive impenetrable unit, it is then that we find help and healing in one another. It is why two is better than one. Not because you have more, but because we have each other. In short, we are one. Always remember this, we are stronger and better when we stand in unity together in the faith. Pastor Cotton got all of his parishioners to safety. When people from the Crescent City asked him how he made it with all of his people, he told them God helped them stay together because as long as they were together, things just kept getting better.

Day 34
"…where two or three are gathered together…" Matt. 18:20

SOMETHING HAS TO HAPPEN

The story was told of the devil sitting outside the church, peeping in and laughing himself to tears. A passerby asked Satan "what he was laughing at?" The devil responded by saying, "They do everything but come together. If they ever came together, something would happen that even I could not stop." Have you ever wondered why there's always some turmoil in the church? It's because if we ever came together, even the devil in hell knows something has to happen. Jesus teaches this same principle like this, "….where two or three are gathered together in my name there will I be in the midst." In other words, God meets us in our unity and kisses it with His supremacy. At that moment, darkness becomes light; sorrow becomes joy; feeble become faithful; and the ordinary becomes extraordinary. Keep this in mind; God is omnipresent. He is everywhere. However, when God's presence produces miracles, healing, and deliverance, that presence is called His gratiosa praesentia. It is His gracious presence, and that occurs when we come together in His name. When we do that in faith, something has to happen.

Day 35
"Come now let us reason together...." Isaiah 1:18

GOD'S GOT THE ANSWERS

To have the support of a church family during a time of crisis can be a blessing. After all, we need each other. But there will always be a time and a season that demands the presence of God. Have you ever been there before? It is the place where you have more hurt than you do healing. It is the moment when you have more doubt than you do belief. It is the season when you are Daniel and in the lion's den. In those times, remember this; God's got the answers. When Isaiah calls Israel to the throne of God, he compels them to come to the sovereign to "...reason together...." The picture is of a child approaching a loving Father with everything because he alone can fix it. If anyone ever tells you they have God all figured out, leave them in a hurry. God permits, allows, and orchestrates human suffering, and there are times when the question marks of life can be overwhelming. In that time, seek the Lord because He can be found. Call upon Him because He is much closer than you could ever imagine. Find your way into His lap with all of your questions because God's got the answers. While you're with God, keep this in mind, just because He's got the answers does not mean He will answer all of your questions. He loves your company, and it took you having questions to get you close to Him.

Day 36
"Wherefore comfort yourselves together...." 1 Thess. 5:11

JUST HELP ME GET THROUGH THIS

One of the reasons God blesses you as a Christian to endure challenging and difficult moments is that He can use you to help others who are going through what you've been through. Who better to help a breast cancer patient than a breast cancer survivor? Who better to encourage a recently divorced believer than another believer who has survived the crucible of divorce? You see, what you have been through was not just for you to make it through but also for the good of others who need to know that God can help them survive and thrive again. When Sister Agnes Ketchings passed away, her children were crushed. Her youngest son took it particularly hard. It brought him to his knees, and he prayed a simple prayer "Lord, just help me get through this!" No sooner than he rose from prayer, his phone rang. It was his best friend whose mother had passed away the year before. The same God that helped his friend was about to help him. When Paul says "....comfort yourselves together..." This is exactly what he means. Let your previous pain become your friends' gain. Use what you have gone through to help another brother or sister.

Day 37
"Can two walk together, except they be agreed" Amos 3:3

GET ON THE GOOD FOOT

Nothing is worse than a marching band in full motion but moving downfield on the wrong foot. It makes you want to shout from the stands, "Left….Left….Left….Left….Left." This way, they can all get on the good foot. You see, the good foot is the foot that your neighbor is marching on. The good foot means being headed in the same direction, moving in the same manner, and marching in step with those you seek to march with. When Amos says, "can two walk together, except they be agreed," he suggests that if you are going right and your brother is going left, there can be no togetherness. Not much will be accomplished if you sing stand-up Saints and your friend sings sit-down Servants. However, we stand united if we are all on the good foot. Here's a great devotional question for you to ponder: who are you marching with these days? What group demands your attention? Who do you find yourself in step with as you walk through life? Birds of a feather flock together. Association brings about assimilation. Walk with those who believe, and you will find yourself walking according to God's Word, which will put you on the good foot every time.

Day 38
"For we are laborers together with God…" 1 Cor. 3:9

WE'VE GOT A LOT OF WORK TO DO

Souls need saving; churches need changing; communities need building; families need strengthening; men need empowering; women need enlightening; married couples need inspiring; single parents need supporting; children need training; fathers need molding; mothers need appreciating; sons need teaching; daughters need instructing; teachers need encouraging; counselors need exhorting; coaches need lifting; administrators need motivating; judges need guiding; lawyers need challenging; doctors need sustaining; city leaders need planning; county commissioners need organizing; national leaders need directing; the sick need healing; the poor need assisting; the elderly need loving; the hungry need feeding; the homeless need housing; the jobless need employing; the lost needs finding; the backslider needs restoring; sinners need redeeming; Pastors need filling; Preachers need a calling; Deacons need informing, and all of God's people need His blessing! If you believe in Jesus Christ, there is no room in the Kingdom of our Lord for just relaxing and doing nothing. We've got a lot of work to do!

Day 39
"Be ye not unequally yoked together...." 2 Cor. 6:14

THANKS, BUT NO THANKS

A young lady was dating a handsome guy that she had long admired. She was a Christian, and he was a church-goer. She was so excited because this was a guy she had longed to get to know. As she got to know him, she noticed differences in their morals, measures, and manners. She quickly noticed something that got on her nerves. Here's what bothered her; in their private time together, he was a touchy, clingy, let's get close, kind of a guy. But, in public, he was extremely "stand-off-ish." After a few weeks with this guy, she concluded they were "unequally yoked." This is a Pauline phrase that suggests that a believer should not look to partner in a relationship with someone who is not a believer. Finally, after getting to know him up close, she made a huge decision, he was good-looking but not good for her. So here's what she did to end the relationship. She sent him a thank you card with a bandaid in it. The card was self-explanatory, but the band-aide made him call to ask what it was for. She told him he had been cut from the program because they were just not made for each other: thanks, but no thanks. Here's the moral of today's lesson, if you're single and searching, look for people who are in love with Him. If they love Him, they have the potential to love you.

Day 40
"...and they sewed fig leaves together..." Gen. 3:7

WE GOT IN TROUBLE TOGETHER

The first time the word "together" is mentioned in the Bible is found in Genesis 3:7. Here is what happened, Adam and Eve did exactly what the Lord told them not to do. When they discovered they were naked, this husband and wife remained united, decided to make something to wear to cover their naked condition, and stitched some fig leaves together. This outfit, as you can imagine, was a complete mess. But we learned at least two things from this troublesome Biblical episode. One, they got in trouble together. Adam could have let Eve stand in her mistake by herself. Adam could have said, "Eve, you are on your own." But he decided to stand with her no matter what. Doesn't this remind you of Jesus? When we have fallen to our lowest, He is still right there. Secondly, they knew that sin needed to be covered. Even though the fig leaves could not do it, they tried to cover their sin. But the blood of the Lamb could handle what the leaves could not do. The blood of the Lamb did not just cover our sins; it cleansed our sins. The moral of this devotional lesson is simply this; we should be so close as Christians that even if we get into trouble, we should find a way to stay together so that nothing tears us apart.

Day 41
"...let us exalt His name together...." Psalms 34:3

YOU'VE GOTTA HELP ME LIFT THIS ONE

The 127th Annual Feast of Our Lady of Mount Carmel and Saint Paulinus of Nola was in full swing in Williamsburg. To capture the celebration up close, a group of strong Italian men placed this statue upon their shoulders to lift him higher. Giglio, as the statue is called, is an 80-foot tall, 3-ton statue. The Giglio is hoisted up by hundreds of strong men and paraded around Havemeyer Street outside the church every year. In a recent celebration, it was said that one strong lifter said to another, "You've gotta help me lift this one!" When David says "....let us exalt His name together..." this is the feeling that he is presenting to the reader. With the exception that David is not referring to an 80-foot statue named Giglio. He refers to an eternal deity named Jehovah, who is God! The Hebrew word exalt comes from the root term room or rum. It means to lift to the highest point possible. This is practically problematic because God is already exalted. God is exalted if you never lift Him at all. So then, how do we lift Him higher? You take everything you are, add it with everything your neighbor is and lift His name as high as possible. In the Toyota Center, where the Rockets play basketball, they have a noise-o-meter. They use it when they want to lift the Rockets, and all of the fans shout. Well, we are not called to lift the Rockets, but we are to lift the name of our Redeemer! His name is Jesus! If you love Him, you've gotta help me lift it!

Day 42
"And let us consider one another..." Heb. 10:24

THE HARSH REALITY OF DISASTER

September 11 is a day that Americans should never forget. On that fateful day, American soil was hit by the worst act of terrorism we have ever seen. Al-Qaeda, led by a very dangerous man Osama bin Laden, who claimed the bombings of the World Trade Centers, and took credit for bombing numerous sites around the U.S. Hundreds went missing, thousands perished, and billions of dollars in infrastructure were destroyed. However, from the disaster and the chaos rose a unity that only a disaster could produce. You see, on September 11th we learned the value of "...considering one another...." Republicans helped Democrats. Atheists helped Hindus. Christians gave a helping hand to Satanists. The Black man helped the White man without considering race, creed, caliber, or color. From the wreckage rose a redemption that only a horrid happening like that could produce. God is a mystery, and today we look back at September 11, 2001, and pose the question: Would it be possible for all of God's creation to live in harmonious resolve as we did on that day? We may not ever know the answer to this query, but we know that to "...consider one another..." is the way of Jesus Christ.

Day 43
"…we shall all be changed…" 1 Cor. 15:51

EVERY BELIEVER, BUT NOT EVERYBODY

While on the subject of being better together, something dynamic comes to mind. It will unfold like a drama on a movie screen. Like a thief in the night, He will sneak into the Earth's atmosphere and snatch the faithful from their perspective places. Two will be asleep in bed, one will be taken, and the other one left. Two will be in the mall shopping, one will be taken and the other one left. Two will be at work in the office, one will be taken and the other one left. Media sources around the world will say that people are missing. Panic will ensue as people try to locate their loved ones. A few people will even be left behind at the church house. They will conclude that Aliens have invaded the Earth from another planet. But nothing will be further from the truth. It will be the rapture of the church of the Living God, by its Living God who promised to return for her. In 1 Corinthians 15, Paul lays out a remarkable theological treatise on the final things and how they will occur. One thing is for sure, it will impact every believer, but not everybody. On that day, the church will stand united, and we shall all be changed!

Day 44
"…we have fellowship one with another…." 1 John 1:7

WHAT A FELLOWSHIP

In 1545, William Turner coined the phrase "birds of a feather flock together." It was a segment of a poetic refrain that he is credited with writing. Nearly a century later, Lucy NaTasha penned the words, "Association brings about assimilation." Though Turner never met Natasha personally, their wisdom brought us a similar truth. When we fellowship, we have things in common that are shared, valued, appreciated, and often celebrated with one another. When John uses the word fellowship, it comes from the Greek term Koinania which means to match or to have in common. In this stead, the fellowship of the saints in the faithful congregation is potent. Believers share the cross, the Word, the Spirit, the love of God, and the labor of the Lord. John writes that when we are in Christ, we have His light, and in that light, we have fellowship with each other. In other words, iron sharpens iron, the picture was painted with the same paintbrush, or united we stand, divided we fall. Take a moment and consider the people that make up your concentric circle of contact and ask yourself this question: Do I share Christ with these people? If not, what's stopping me? If so, what's blessing me? Keep this in mind. The fellowship that you share in Christ with Christians will last you forever!

Day 45
"Exhort one another daily...." Heb. 3:13

LET ME ENCOURAGE YOU

There is a beautiful story written in 1 Samuel 30:6-8 where a horrible crisis hits King David, and finds a way to encourage himself in the Lord. However, there are days, times, and seasons when life can hit you so hard that it becomes nearly impossible for you to encourage yourself. You need someone else to do it for you. Let's be clear; it's not like you are walking around with a huge sign on your forehead that says, "Will somebody please encourage me?" But that is how you feel deep within. At that moment, you began to realize the benefit of having someone to encourage you! The term exhort used in this passage means to strongly encourage someone. It was primarily used on the battlefield between soldiers right after a battle and before the next. The word "courage" means the will to fight on. So to be encouraged means to be ready to keep going no matter what. If you are a believer in Jesus Christ, you have a job to do for God: find the heart of a fellow believer. Take a few moments and tell them, "I'm just here to encourage you!"

Day 46
"...and they gave to me...the right hand of fellowship..." Gal. 2:9

THE RIGHT HAND OF FELLOWSHIP

Every denomination has within its confines doctrines and dogmas that are practiced. Many of these practices have nothing to do with salvation but everything to do with proper protocol for an established body of believers. With this in mind, traditional Baptists would strongly enforce "the right hand of fellowship." If you were raised in the Baptist Church, the only way to become a church member was to confess belief in a resurrected redeemer, get baptized in water through total immersion, take your first communion and receive the "right hand of fellowship" by the Pastor. What was the meaning of this? It was an outward sign of our inward commitment to Christ, His teachings, and His work together for those who believe in Him. When Paul writes the letter to the churches of Galatia, some people had walls of religious tradition that kept certain people away from God. These people were called Judaizers. They wanted you to keep the law and circumcision. But, there was a new system of belief being presented. The one that came from Christ through Paul called grace! When Peter embraced this grace, he extended to Paul and those with him the "right hand of fellowship." It was their way of saying if this grace is true, I want some too! As you share with other believers and shake their hands, remember this, it is a sign of fellowship and not just a handshake. It symbolizes that we both need God's grace to make it.

Day 47
"And have no fellowship with the unfruitful works of darkness…"   Eph. 5:11

RUN FOREST, RUN

Have you seen the Grammy Award-winning movie starring Tom Hanks called Forrest Gump? If you haven't, then shame on you. But, if you have, you know well that the title of this devotional lesson comes from the advice that Jenny gave Forrest whenever he faced tight spots and challenging times. Jenny said, "Run, Forrest, run." As believers in Jesus Christ, we are instructed to have "…no fellowship with the unfruitful works of darkness…." Any activity that does not produce the fruitful works of Jesus Christ in the light is the unfruitful works of darkness. Worthless works are those things that we should avoid. Run from wrongdoings of the flesh, sins of the tongue, and the appearance of evil. Run from people who will celebrate your sin and become frustrated when you seek to serve the Lord. And, run from anyone who does not want you to be closer to Jesus Christ in walk, talk, and personal witness. You know, when Forrest ran, God blessed him. He ran on the football field and he ran into a Medal of Honor. Running blessed him. The same is true for you! When it comes to works of darkness, run, child of God, run!

Day 48
"…but when He had put them all out…." Mark 5:40

ATTENDANCE IS ONE THING; AGREEMENT IS ANOTHER

Let's just set the record straight. Just because people are in attendance does not mean they agree. Some people are present to spectate. They want to see what is going on. Others are there to instigate. They want to push an agenda that has nothing to do with the real needs being met. But, what is needed is a handful of true believers that are present that can prayerfully participate. Jesus, in this story, is in the house of Jarius, and a twelve-year-old child has been pronounced dead. But Jesus shows up, puts the people in attendance out, and removes them from the premises. Why does He do this? He does this not to be mean, harsh, or indignant. But, He does so because they are in attendance and not in agreement. The Lord is still a miracle worker! But, some people near you could hinder what the Lord is about to do in your life. Here's a great devotional question to consider. Are the people nearest you right now merely in attendance, or are they in agreement? If they are just in attendance, they want to see what's happening in your life. But, if they are in agreement, they will stand in faith and believe God with you for the needs that you have and the prayers that you pray. As believers in Jesus Christ, when we stand in agreement together, miracles still happen because our God is still a miracle worker.

Day 49
"...that I may know Him...and the fellowship of His sufferings..."   Psalms 34:3

IT'S THE TRADEMARK

A trademark is best defined as a symbol, word, or phrase attributed to an entity or individual that stamps what they are and what they produce as authentic. The trademark for Lexus is the coveted circled capital letter L. The trademark for Louis Vuitton is the matchless symbol LV. And the trademark for Cadillac is the marvelous symbol of the crescent crown. Trademarks mean everything. It separates items that are real from those that are fictitious. When you think about the trademark of a Christian, what comes to your mind? Singing, speaking in tongues, quoting scripture from memory, perhaps? Here's the truth, none of those things are marks of authenticity for the believer who loves the Lord. Our trademark is sharing in "...the fellowship of His sufferings...." God allows His children to suffer because His Son, our Savior, suffered while on Earth. It is the place where we share with God and each other. We all will see seasons of human suffering. God permits it because suffering is not meant to destroy you but to develop you. Our fellowship with Christ and each other says we may suffer, but we still love God.

Day 50
"And they continued steadfastly in....fellowship...." Acts 2:42

ONE SIZE FITS ALL

Don't you hate hearing it? One size fits all. It's almost never true. Somebody is always too big or too small, too short or too tall. It just isn't true in most cases. However, this is one place where "one size does fit all." It is where we Christians come together regardless of race, creed, color, caliber, or socio-economic context. It is the space where believers join themselves with other saints, all for the purpose of knowing that all of us have sinned in one way or another, but the God of all grace has granted each of us another opportunity to live for Him. In this stead, "one size does fit all." In a theological sense, this is called the place of provisional grace. It is what we all need to survive. When Luke writes Acts 2:42, Christians are being persecuted and threatened on every hand. But what helped them push forward regardless of the human hurt they encountered was that they gained strength from each other in fellowship. Here's a solid question to consider as we share this devotional moment; what believers do you gain strength from and why? Hold on to this truth. Everybody needs somebody. In this regard, "one size fits all."

Day 51
"So built we the wall...." Neh. 4:6a

WE, WE AIN'T ALWAYS FRENCH

When Nehemiah says, "...so built we the wall..." he is not speaking French. Look closely at the spelling in the passage. It is not "Oui" but "We." When the people of God unite, there's nothing we cannot do or accomplish with faith in almighty God. The problem is that we live in a culture filled with people who have bought into a "Do It Yourselfers" philosophy. Here's the truth, there are some things that cannot be done alone. It requires the help, friendship, partnership, and presence of others to share the work with you to accomplish a specific goal. Nehemiah is about to rebuild the city's walls that had been previously destroyed. It had been said that he could not do it, and if he attempted to build it, his construction efforts would be weak and futile. But, what his enemies did not count on was the people that would come together to lend a hand in rebuilding the wall. At the Antioch Church, we have experienced such a phenomenon. We came together and, with faith in God, liquidated a debt of 14.6 million dollars in the fall of 2022. And in the fall of 2023, we stood with God and watched Him pay off a $7.4 million debt on our Youth and Children's Complex. While churches across the country were closing, we stood with Christ and watched Him give us the strength to expand. This only happened because we were together in the faith of the Lord Jesus Christ together.

Day 52
"If my people...." 1 Chron. 7:14

WE THE PEOPLE

The first three words of the preamble to the Constitution of the United States of America read on this wise, "We the people...." The founders of this country knew and understood that there would always be power in the people's hearts. When you read the words of 1 Chronicles 7:14, it is as if Solomon had the same thing in mind. For he begins this verse by giving quotes from God to God's people regarding what they should do when problems arise, issues confront them, and life starts to fall apart. Here's what the Lord instructs His people to do. He says, "If my people who are called by my name shall humble themselves and pray....." You see, "we the people" is the centerpiece of a movement with God as its raison d'etre. In this stead, there are times when we pray by ourselves, and there is nothing wrong with that. In fact, there is power in praying to God as a child of the King. But, something supernatural comes to pass when the people of God pray together. Here's the truth, any group that prays together will see God's power manifest together: a family, a team, a company, or a church. Group prayer says, "...we the people..." can connect to the God who has all power. With this in mind, when was the last time you attended a prayer meeting, shared a prayer call, or prayed with a group of believers? If you have not done so lately, you should! "We, the people," can still move God when we pray.

Day 53
"And Miriam....took a timbrel in her hand..." Ex. 15:20
DON'T LET ME SHOUT BY MYSELF

When Moses and the children of Israel crossed the Red Sea, it was more than just a miracle. It was a move of God. The Lord blocked the Egyptians' advance so they could not get to His children. He then caused a strong east wind to blow all night until the sea was opened, and they walked across on dry ground while the water from the sea stood like decorative water walls around them. When the last Egyptian made his way to the other side, the water of the Red Sea collapsed on Pharaoh and his entire Army. It was then that Miriam, Moses's sister, grabbed a tambourine and started to dance, shout and celebrate! The good news is that as she celebrated, the women of Israel decided that she should not celebrate alone, so they joined her in praising God. The worship of our God can come from the soul of one believer. However, the praise of our God often requires an assembly of saints that can join in exalting the Lord for what He has done and is currently doing. When worship happens in a corporate setting, what do you usually do? Do you sit and observe? Do you actively participate? Do you wait to see what others will do and then decide how you will respond? Whatever the case, everyone should share the public celebration of what God has done!

Day 54
"Therefore is the name of it called Babel...." Gen. 11:9
THE POSSIBILITIES ARE ENDLESS

We have been studying what the Bible says about unity, synergy, harmony, oneness, and togetherness for about two months. And it is clear that when we unite and unify ourselves, the sky's the limit. We usually make this statement figuratively rather than literally. But what if there was a story in the Bible that would suggest that if we came together on Earth, the potential of humankind, coupled with the creativity that the Creator placed in us, could reach beyond the skies into the heavens? Let's consider the story of the Tower of Babel recorded in Genesis 11. It is one of the most seldom taught narratives of the Bible because it seems so senseless to think that people could build a tower high enough to reach the dwelling place of God. And, it seems so much like "make believe" that God would confound and confuse human language because for humanity to achieve such would be impossible. Yet the people of the Earth all speak different languages, so we continue to "Babel." The presence of this story is given in scripture not just to show us where various languages derived from but to give details and descriptions of the fact that we can reach beyond the sky if we ever come together. It is why the devil works so arduously to ensure that we don't because even he knows that the possibilities would be endless.

Day 55
"....forsake not the assembling of yourselves together" Hebrews 10:25

AND YOU'RE GOING TO CHURCH

These were words that many of us were raised hearing. They fell from the lips of family matriarchs regarding the worship of our God on the eight day of the week, according to the Christian Sabbath, Sunday morning. You see, it does not matter how late you were out or how busy you'd become during the week. On a Sunday morning, you were going to church. In fact, for those who were raised in the tradition of "church," you know that church lasted the entire day. Sunday School was at 9:30 am, and morning worship lasted from 11:00 am to nearly 2:00 pm. Stay close because the 3:00 pm service was going to begin in just a moment, and from that service would come Baptist Training Union (BTU) from 5:00 pm to 6:00 pm. And finally, the evening service would start at 7:00 pm. Why so much church? The saints of old knew that there was power in fellowship and togetherness. There was meaning and purpose in our praise songs, hymns, and prayers. There was enlightenment, empowerment, and enrichment in our time hearing God's Word taught and preached. The Bible says, "Faith cometh by hearing and hearing by the Word of God." Make up your mind right now that you will let nothing keep you from attending church! It's the place and people you gain your strength from.

Day 56
"…and he that soweth discord among the brethren…" Prov. 6:19

BUT SOME PEOPLE ARE JUST MESSY

Yes, the Bible says Christians should dwell together in unity, stand together in the faith, and fight together for the faith. However, how do you handle standing with other believers you find it hard to stand together with? Here's the same thing put a different way. Some people can be hard, difficult, and even impossible to partner with. For instance, have you ever had to work with someone who was just messy? Someone who always had the latest hot gossip on everyone else but no news on themselves. It can ruin the Spirit of togetherness in about 30 seconds. The Proverbial writer gives us some insight into the people that even God does not particularly care for. Of course, God hates all sin and loves all sinners. However, some issues can just run God hot. One is a person who "…sows discord among the brethren…." A person who works to divide us rather than bring us together. A person who is busy being bitter about what exists instead of working faithfully to make it better for everyone involved. Let's be nice to messy people for a moment because none of us are perfect. This note is for all the really messy people reading this devotional lesson right now. We love you, but we hate the division your "messy" causes. So we have a special favor to ask of you. Please stop it! Any Kingdom divided against itself cannot stand.

Day 57
"…the Lord spake unto Joshua…" Joshua 1:1

YOU DON'T HAVE TO TRY TO RUN EVERYTHING

Have you ever tried working with someone that had to run the whole show? Of course, we need leadership and guidance to have organization and structure. And, yes, we must have responsible people in charge that can help move everything forward for the cause of Christ. However, some people have to be in charge. They have to let everyone know that it's them running the show. In some cases, it is a Pastor that cannot deal with private inadequacies and insufficiencies; therefore, everything has to come through his office. But it doesn't have to be a Pastor. It could be anyone in a group that makes life difficult for everyone else because they have to have things done their way. One of the most amazing things about the story of Joshua found in scripture is that he was there with Moses the whole time. He did not try to dominate. He did not spectate from the sideline while hoping for a leadership position to surface so that he could have an opportunity to be in charge. Joshua let his service speak for him. The truth of the matter is that you really shouldn't care who scores the touchdown as long as your team wins! You don't have to run it when you are there to help it.

Day 58
"If a man say, I love God and hateth his brother he is a liar…" 1 John 4:20

DON'T GET CAUGHT IN A LIE

To say you love the Lord is one thing. But, to say you hate anyone that the Lord made makes you a liar. When we encounter difficult people up close, we quickly show our discontent. Moreover, when we know hateful, mean, evil, messy people, it is our natural reaction to give them back what they have given us. However, please hear this; such is not the way of God. Okay, let's clear the air before you put down your devotional guide. You may hate the wrong that they've done or strongly dislike their character and actions. But it is not okay for you to hate them. If you say, "I love the Lord and hate them," you do not love God. This is a strong language written by John here in this verse. To love God is to love others. This does not mean that you have some warm fuzzy feeling on the inside. It does not mean that you want to hug them and sing fireside songs. What it does mean is that you have made a decision to love God, and that decision makes other decisions for you to include loving people that are hard for you to love. The real root of unity is not seen in how many people you can love that you like. It is seen in how you, as a Christian, can love those that do not love or like you. Hear these words and let them rest in the resonance of your human soul. Don't get caught in a lie!

Day 59
"...bringing one sick of the palsy which was borne by four..." Mark 2:4

JUST DO YOUR PART

Mark chapter two opens with a story that demands our attention. Jesus is in a city called Capernaum. He is in a house teaching and doing what He does. These four guys carry their friend who is sick of the palsy and cannot walk to Him. There is so much that we do not know about this story. For instance, we do not know anyone's name. We do not know where they came from, and we do not know how they got the news that Jesus was in town. We do not know how far they had to walk, and we do not know how much their friend weighed. You know dead weight is heavier to carry in most cases. We do not know what the man being carried was like. We do not know if he was hopeful, fretful, hateful, or joyful. We know that to get their friend to Jesus Christ, they each had to do their part. They each had to hold up their end. They each had to walk at a steady pace so that their friend would not hit the ground. They each had to adjust their attitude because it was likely really hot while they were walking. And we do know that when they got to the house where Jesus was located, they tore the roof off to get their friend the help he needed from Jesus Christ. You see, the four men carrying the load had to do their part to see healing happen for those they loved. Here's the bottom line, when you do your part, healing happens for those who need it most.

Day 60
"And they beckoned unto their partners...." Luke 5:11

WHEN HELPING ME BLESSES YOU

Often when we help people in a time of need, it is an act of kindness extended toward them with no thought of recompense or repayment in mind. So we help people expecting nothing back from them, but perhaps a simple thank you at most. But what if it were possible to help in such a way that it blesses you in return? Would you do it? Here's the same question phrased a different way. Would you be interested if you were told that there was a way to help others and incredibly bless yourself in the process? If you answered yes, please know this devotional lesson and Biblical story are for you. In Luke 5, we find the narrative where Peter fished all night and caught nothing. He had decided to quit and call it a day. Jesus said, "Let down your nets for a drought." Peter let down one net, which became so full of fish that the nets started breaking. His only hope was to call some friends to come and help him. Peter had so many fish when they got there, it is starting to sink both boats. Both boats started empty and ended up full. If his friends had not come to help him, their boat would have remained empty. As a believer in Jesus Christ, you do not bless people to get a blessing. You bless people because God has blessed you!

Day 61
"So the last shall be first…." Matthew 20:16

LAST BUT NOT LEAST

The heart of a servant can often put you in last place. While you serve others, sometimes your needs need to be met. While you sacrifice for others, there are times when it seems as if no one sacrifices for you. There are times and seasons when it seems rather foolish to put others first because many of the people you have sacrificed to help never even bother to stop and say thank you. Here's a probing interrogative for you to consider as we share this moment. Have you ever felt completely unappreciated? Have you ever felt that your humility had been taken for stupidity? Have you ever reached a point where you became selfish and said, "I don't care about them anymore. I'm going to take care of me, myself, and I?" In moments like these, a moment of Kingdom reflection is most beneficial. You see, God has this fascinating habit. He exalts people who humble themselves. He lifts people to higher heights without going through the channels of proper protocol. He even does the unthinkable. He takes the people who voluntarily placed themselves in last place and put them in first place. Serving can seem like you're in last place, but a promotion is coming that puts you at the top!

Day 62
"…and all of the members of that body being one body…." 1 Cor. 12:12

MEMBERSHIP HAS ITS PRIVILEGES

In the Summer of 1979, something extraordinary happened in northeast Houston. A new YMCA was constructed and opened for business. To be a member meant everything because membership had its privileges. There was swimming, baseball, basketball, flag football, ping pong, soccer, and so on. In many instances, being a church member is looked upon like being a member of the local YMCA. However, nothing could be further from the truth. When the Apostle Paul presents the idea of membership, he is doing so with a physical body in mind, each part of the body fulfilling a necessary function. In this way, if you are a Christian and a believer in Jesus Christ, you are a member with great privileges. What privilege do you ask? The honor of being attached to the one true and Living God. You may not ever have a title, but you matter. Your name may not ever be called, but you are a vital part of the body of Christ. Think of it this way, if you could be a part of the greatest organization time has ever seen, wouldn't you be proud of that? Likewise, as a believer in Christ Jesus, your membership is privileged because you are attached to Him.

Day 63
"Now concerning spiritual gifts…." 1 Cor. 12:1

USE YOUR GIFTS FOR GOOD

The church of God on Earth does not suffer or struggle because it is not gifted. We struggle because we have yet to learn the value of using our gifts for good. To make matters worse, we often delete and destroy gifts we do not understand or comprehend. We fear some gifts, so we never seek to use them. Imagine, for a moment, the giftedness of the fastest sprinter that ever lived, Usain Bolt, trying to run with one leg. Imagine the greatest boxer of all time, Floyd "Big Money" Mayweather, only using one arm. These images may seem silly, but it's exactly what the church looks like trying to do Kingdom work without using all its giftedness. The Apostle Paul, in the passage listed above, is emphatically clear about the presence and potency of spiritual gifts. The Holy Spirit gives these gifts to the body of Christ to energize and empower it for service on Earth. Jesus said, "And greater works shall you do because I go unto the Father." Here's a great devotional question for you to ponder, what gift do you possess that is not currently being used in the body of Christ? Keep this in mind. The church wins every time we use our gifts for good.

Day 64
"But by the Holy Ghost…." 1 Cor. 12:4c

WE HAVE A GHOST

The hottest mode of this new television age is, without a doubt, Netflix. The channel is well known for its movie previews and series presentations that capture audiences worldwide. They have a new show running entitled "We Have A Ghost!" Even though it's running on Netflix, it's been true since Pentecost for the church of the Living God. Friends, we have a Ghost. He is not some figment of our imagination. He is the third person of the Godhead, co-equal to God the Father and God the Son. The Holy Spirit is the true inspiration of the church. And, it is the Holy Spirit that indwells true believers to become witnesses for the Lord and produce workers that serve God by serving others, using spiritual gifts for the glory of God. The Apostle Paul presents a beautiful portrait of how the spiritual gifts in the body of Christ come through the person of the Holy Ghost. Something extraordinary occurs when He, the Holy Ghost, has free course. He causes the giftedness within the body of Christ to spring forth and live in the people of God. In short, we have a Ghost, and for believers in the Lord, He is the Holy Ghost. Have you ever encountered Him? Do you know Him?

Day 65
"But it is the same God that worketh all in all...." 1 Cor. 12:6

YOU'RE AN ACTOR, BUT IT'S HIS PRODUCTION

The silver screen captures moviegoers' attention from border to border and sea to sea. Even though every move is different, there is at least one similarity. Actors are not always producers. You see, the person responsible for the entire production is the risk taker, money manager, and decision maker. Actors are employed through agencies by the producer to do the work so that the result is a great new movie. This is precisely how the Kingdom of God on Earth works. As a believer in the Lord Jesus Christ, you are empowered by the Holy Ghost like an actor on a stage. In this stead, we play our part. When our role is over, our life ends. The movie keeps going until the rapture happens. The reason for this is simple. It is His production. The best way to put this is to say it like this, "but it is the same God that worketh all in all...." In other words, it is all about the producer. He writes the script. He assigns the parts. He directs the affairs of the production. He makes the changes. He ensures that things are going according to scale. With this in mind, walk through life, moving forward by faith, embracing every moment, knowing it is all about the Producer because you're an actor.

Day 66
"...by the Spirit the Word of Wisdom...." 1 Cor. 12:8a

WORD TO THE WISE

The Greek word for wisdom is the term Sophia. It is like the lady's name in the film The Color Purple, Harpo's wife, played by Oprah Winfrey. Sophia! Sophia! Sophia! It is best defined as the gifted ability to know what to do, when to do it, and how to do it, with the faith to get it done. Even more meaningful in that wisdom is one of the most powerful gifts of the Spirit we could ever encounter. In 1 Cor. 12:8a, as Paul begins sharing spiritual gifts with the Church at Corinth, "...the word of wisdom..." is gift number one. Oftentimes, wisdom is attributed to those who are older because life has taught them some lessons from the school of hard knocks. Those lessons, taught and learned, produced wisdom. With this in mind, we can often receive a "word to the wise." Keep this in mind; nothing outranks wisdom on Earth. In short, wisdom wins every time. A wise principal will have the best school. A wise coach will have a winning team. A wise mother will have great children. A wise father will have a blessed family. A wise CEO will have a profitable company. A wise Pastor will have an obedient, faithful church. Here's a great word to the wise as you share this devotional: "Seek God, find wisdom, choose wisely. The choices that you make in life will determine the quality of life you live."

Day 67
"....the Word of Knowledge...." 1 Cor. 12:8b

I KNOW WHAT I'M TALKING ABOUT

John Alexander is an experienced trucker who has been driving eighteen-wheelers from coast to coast in America for over two decades. When it comes to trucking, if you hear him say, "I know what I'm talking about," it means that he knows. His skillset comes from book knowledge, academic pedagogy, and years of experience on the road. Imagine God saying, "I know what I'm talking about." In this sense, this is what the word knowledge means. It comes from the Greek term "gnosis," which suggests somewhere in the laboratory, a scientist discovered an irrefutable and undeniable fact. Please hear this; God knows! The awesome news in 1 Cor. 12:8 is that all knowledge has a source. For the believer in Jesus Christ, the source of what we know comes from Him. In this stead, "...the word of knowledge..." radically changes what we believe, and what we believe alters how we behave. Knowledge as a spiritual gift looks like Noah building an Ark with no rain and no engineering degree. He has limited experience with the animals on his boat and how to care for them. Where did his knowledge come from, you ask? It came from God. When God says, "I know what I'm talking about." You might want to believe Him!

Day 68
"...to another faith...." 1 Cor. 12:9a

CRAZY FAITH

There are dimensions of faith given in the scriptures. There is "the measure of faith" given to everyone. There is weak faith. This is the kind of faith that the Disciples of Jesus often put on display. There is saving faith. This faith is strong enough to place belief in our risen Redeemer, Jesus Christ, needed for salvation. There is great faith. This kind of faith describes the woman in Mark 5 that touched the garment of Jesus and was made whole of her plague. But then, there is crazy faith! This is the faith of the men in Mark 2 that carry their friend in Capernaum, and when they got there, even though the house was packed, they tore the roof off of the house to get to Jesus. As Paul writes the Corinthians about spiritual gifts, at the top of his list is "....faith...." Remember that faith and belief are two sides of the same coin. With this in mind, you cannot have faith in something you do not believe in. Faith then acts on what belief asserts is true. In Luke 17, we see what crazy faith looks like. Ten men filled with leprosy cry out to Jesus for healing, and He sends them to the priest in the city. And, as they go, physical restoration starts to take place. They believe the Lord in His word. Proof of their belief was that they had the faith to start walking. The Bible then gives this incredible report, "...as they went, they were made whole." Crazy faith equals amazing grace! You cannot have one without the other.

Day 69
"…gifts of healing…." 1 Cor. 12:9b

WHEN HEALING HAPPENS

Gifts of healing have, by some, been frowned upon. The atheist calls it luck. The mystic calls it good fortune. The agnostic calls it foolishness. And many Scientologists think we have lost our minds even to consider such truth. But here's the amazing report from the scriptures, God still can and still does various acts of healing every day. The word healing used by Paul in his list of spiritual gifts in 1 Cor. 12 is "therapuzo," which means to restore. It was used to describe the broken bone of a soldier that had been put back in place and mended over time. The spiritual gift of healing refers to healing that can be instant or restored over time. In either instance, God receives the glory from the healing that has taken place. By the way healing can take place at any time. It occurs when what was was broken is repaired and restored, no matter how God chooses to do it. In this way, God heals through medicine. God heals through herbal supplements. God heals through counselors. God heals through prayer and the laying on of hands. The vital part of this lesson is to know and believe that any time healing takes place, God did it! God is responsible for it! God structured its occurrence so that it could happen and restoration could be yours! What does healing look like? Find a mirror and give it a stare.

Day 70
"….to another miracles…." 1 Cor. 12:10a

MIRACLES STILL HAPPEN

Unlike healing, miracles are always eventful and instant. Healing can happen over a period of time and have a miraculous outcome. But, when it comes to miracles, they are eventful and instant. It is something that happens in the ever-present now, and its outcomes are beyond explanation through the power and presence of the Holy Spirit. The tires from the Toyota Corolla screamed as the brake was applied with mad force. Black smoke filled the air on the I-45 Northbound corridor. In just seconds, a huge truck pulling a forty-foot gooseneck trailer slammed into the rear of the small Corolla and rolled onto its roof. In short, the huge truck pulling the trailer ran over the car. Screams and the horrid sound of smashing metal filled the atmosphere. Pedestrians from other vehicles soon stopped, and the freeway was filled with cars and trucks going nowhere. A short sandy-haired Hispanic lady exited her car, walked over to the smashed Toyota, fell on her knees, and prayed. She stood up with a smile on her face and said, "Everyone will survive. It is all okay." Emergency response crews showed up with the jaws of life. The driver of the huge truck was fine. But the people in the Toyota were presumed dead or seriously injured. When the EMS crew cut the car open, four people all crawled out with just minor injuries. The man holding the saw said, "Somebody here has to know God. This is a miracle!" He then explained that the engine from the car was sitting in the front seat, and the trunk was in the back seat, leaving no room for survivors. The Hispanic lady said, "…miracles still happen."

Day 71
"…to another prophecies…." 1 Cor. 12:10b

TOMORROW'S NEWS TODAY

Prophecy is best defined as tomorrow's news today. It occurs when the Holy Spirit reveals to a believer the future of a particular thing, and they can tell you what will happen before it occurs. One of the most awe-inspiring portraits of prophecy given in the Bible took place in 2 Chronicles 20 when Jehosophat is about to be attacked by a host of his enemies that he could have destroyed when he was younger. While seated on his throne, a young man, whose name is Jahaziel had been moved by the spirit of the Lord, declared to him the battle he thought would be his did not belong to him. Jahaziel then told the King exactly what to do to come out of the battle victorious. King Jehosophat obeys by faith, and the result was amazing! The people of God win the fight without ever lifting their fists because the prophecy that had been delivered was true. When Paul says "…to other prophecies…" he is saying that some in the body possess this gift. Remember this, real "prophets" do not use their gifts for "profits." They use their gifts for God's glory and our good.

Day 72
"…to another the discerning of spirits…." 1 Cor. 12:10c

SHE READ HIM LIKE A BOOK

The spiritual gift of "discerning of spirits" takes place when the Holy Spirit empowers those in the body of Christ with the clarity to see spiritually into the lives of those He seeks to heal. In Acts 16, Paul and Silas are in Philippi, and a girl with an evil spirit follows them. Paul could discern her Spirit and set the girl free. In 1981 four boys riding their bikes through a neighborhood in northeast Houston decided to stop on Mesa Road at a church called New Day. The saints were in worship, and a lady walked to the back and asked if she could pray with a young man named Ricky Hebert. She had him lift his hands, and she spoke boldly to him these words. She said, "You have the hands of a rich man, but you steal, don't you?" He said, "Yes." To which she replied, "Steal no longer." She said, "You came in here because you want to know God, don't you?" He again replied, "Yes." She said, "You are known for fighting, aren't you?" Ricky began weeping uncontrollably and said again, "Yes." She said, "You will no longer fight and beat people. God has other plans for you." What was it young Ricky Hebert encountered, you ask? It was the gift of the discerning spirits. Be careful! Not everyone speaking to you has this gift or is led by God. But when the Lord leads them, they are gifted to help you heal because God has work for you to do.

Day 73
"…to another divers kinds of tongues…." 1 Cor. 12:10d

TONGUES

The gift of tongues is, without a doubt, a spiritual gift. Some contend that this gift and others existed earlier but no longer exist today. Here's the truth, the gift of tongues operates today under the auspices of the Holy Ghost. It is not a prayer language, as some suppose. After all, what language can you speak to God that He, who knows all things, does not understand? Here's the truth: it is a gift graced by God to those in the body of Christ to exhort the heart of the one who has the gift. When Paul teaches about spiritual gifts in 1 Corinthians, tongues are at the bottom of the list. This signifies a gift from the Holy Spirit that does not carry the same weight as those mentioned earlier. But they do carry the same source, which is God Himself. With this being said, the gift of tongues takes place when the Lord deems it necessary for those He chooses. It is a beautiful gift. It is a very personal gift. It is a gift of passion and can be used in various ways to strengthen the individual, who, in turn, empowers the body of Christ. Quick question, "have you ever encountered someone who speaks in tongues?" What was your first thought? Do you have the gift of tongues? How do you use it, and when?

Day 74
"…to another the interpretation of tongues…." 1 Cor. 12:10e

SOMEBODY TELL ME WHAT THEY JUST SAID

The worship service was filled with the presence of God. It was evident that the Holy Spirit was with His people then. Suddenly, a woman jumped to her feet in the cathedral's rear and spoke aloud in tongues. While she was speaking, a man up front leaped to his feet and started preaching. When the woman would stop speaking, the man would stop preaching. And, when the woman commenced with speaking, the man would commence with preaching. It was then that the Pastor declared that what had just taken place was the use of the interpretation of tongues. Paul is so ordered on spiritual gifts in 1 Corinthians 12 that it is hard to misunderstand him. In this way, tongues are a spiritual gift, but because no one can understand it when used, they should come with the interpretation of tongues by someone else. When this happens, not only is the person speaking in tongues edified, but the entire body of Christ present is edified because they have seen and heard God work in the company of the saved.

Day 75
"...dividing to every man severally as he will...." 1 Cor. 12:11

FOR OUR GOOD AND HIS GLORY

Imagine God sitting on His throne with His majestic head bowed in disgust. Imagine splendid angelic beings flying around Him, trying to encourage Him. One angel finally asked Him, "Sovereign God, what seems to be the problem?" He replies, "I have gone through a lot of trouble to bless My people with gifts from Me, and they have no idea what they are or how I want them to use them." Spiritual gifts that reside in the hearts of God's people are designed to empower the people for administration, appeal, and service. In short, spiritual gifts are for our good and His glory. God does not grace us with His gifts just for us. They are really for Him. Be sure to understand that these gifts we have studied over the last couple of days are just that...they are gifts. You may ask the Lord for any gift of your choosing. But just because you ask does not mean that the gift of your request will be granted. In other words, spiritual gifts come at the mercy of the one who grants them. For the believer in Christ, that someone is the Lord our God. The amazing news about using spiritual gifts is that everyone in the body of Christ has a gift to use. It is why you are present. If you do not know your gifts, you must take a spiritual gifts inventory test, discover and use it.

Day 76
"For the body is not one member but many...." 1 Cor. 12:14

TEAMWORK MAKES THE DREAM WORK

The physical anatomy is a miraculous machine created by God made of ten incredible systems that work together as a team. The skeletal, muscular, nervous, endocrine, cardiovascular, lymphatic, respiratory, digestive, urinary, and reproductive systems make the body function. Each system works in harmony with the others so that the result is a body that functions properly and stays alive. Every system wants to avoid overrunning or doing away with an existing system. This would be bio-internal chaos. The Lord created these systems to work as a team. In this stead, teamwork does make the dream work. No system alone can keep the body alive, and when one system fails, it causes a burden on the other systems that exist. Like a physical body, Paul teaches the Corinthian Christians that the same is true with the church. We are one body, but we have many parts. These parts cause us to function like we are one body. In this way, cooperation is how our biological systems exist. The administration is what takes place when they synergistically perform their established functions. Most importantly, health and harmony are what we get when the body works together for our good. It is teamwork at its best that makes the dream work nonetheless.

Day 77
"…if the foot shall say I am not the hand…." 1 Cor. 12:15

I'M WAITING ON YOU HAND AND FOOT

Please take a moment to read 1 Corinthians 12:15. It may seem somewhat ridiculous, but the truth is that both the hand and the foot are necessary. Without your hands, your ability to maneuver, manipulate, and ever manufacture would be greatly hindered, if not impossible. Without your feet, you could not stand, run, walk, or be mobile without assistance. With this in mind, there is no time for the hand and foot to get into an altercation because one feels more important than the other. They are both equally important because they are members of the same body and play an essential role in the total health of the anatomy. Likewise, when we look at the body of Christ, called the church, we must conclude that such is the truth for the church. Every ministry construct that makes up the local assembly that empowers us to fulfill the Great Commission and the Great Commandment is critically essential. With this in mind, when the body of Christ on Earth embraces our uniqueness and celebrates our similarities, we can fall on the throne of our Master and Lord and say with humility: "I'm Waiting On You Hand And Foot!"

Day 78
"…if the ear shall say because I am not the eye…." 1 Cor. 12:16

EARS AND EYES

They are the two most vital parts of the facial structure known to every human being on the planet. With these two elements come vision and vitality. Through these two portals come to sight and sound. They are your eyes and ears. And even though they are crucial and critical, they are not the body's most essential structures. Living without sight and sound is possible, plausible, and achievable. However, you cannot live without lungs, a heart, a pancreas, or a liver. Here's the point, no matter how important your hearing and seeing may be, the body still needs its other elements to function for the body to remain alive and strong. This is what the Apostle Paul is teaching the church at Corinth when he shares these ideas regarding the physical body vis a vis the body of Christ. The ear cannot say because I am not the eye; I am not important. And the eye cannot say to the ear, "I don't need you." The point here is that every part of Christ's body matters. We often need to pay more attention to the importance of those who are not seen or heard, thinking that their roles are less than others. However, nothing could be further from the truth. Every member matters to the Lord!

Day 79
"...if the whole body were an eye...." 1 Cor. 12:17
EYES ARE IMPORTANT, BUT THEY'RE NOT EVERYTHING

In his book 40 Days In The Word, Rick Warren made an interesting argument about how we can interpret scripture to learn and grow from it. In this stead, Warren contends that one great way to learn and grow in God's Word is to picture it. That is to say, take a moment after reading a passage in the Bible and then activate the virtual cortex of your brain, pull on your imagination, and do your best to picture it. Try to imagine what the verse looks like. With this in mind, Read 1 Corinthians 12:17 and try to picture it. Did what you imagine scare you just a little bit? It could have. Think of it...one giant eyeball! Paul is making one emphatic point here, and it is this, eyes are important, but they are not everything. To help prove his point, Paul paints a picture of the eye being everything, and it makes no sense at all. There would be no walking, talking, breathing, eating, chewing, hearing, or living. The eye alone is not a body. The eye alone will never be able to do everything a body does. The eyes are vital, but the rest of the body plays a role and has a place in the body's overall health. Take a moment and look at the role you play within the body of Christ at your church. Now keep this in mind; your name may never be called. Your face may never be seen. But, the work you do as a member is equally as important as the others in the body.

Day 80
"...charity....charity....charity....charity....charity..." 1 Cor. 13
LOVE NEVER LOSES

Spiritual gifts in the body of Christ are extremely important. Without these gifts, the church cannot fulfill the mandates the Lord has set before us. However, there is something greater than spiritual gifts. It is more important than wisdom, knowledge, faith, administration, prophecy, tongues, the interpretation of tongues, or any other gift in the scriptures. This one element is so much more important than the spiritual gifts listed in the Bible until God refers to Himself as this one thing. In other words, there is something that outranks spiritual gifts. There is something more important to God than spiritual gifts. This could be really upsetting to people pushed by gifts, titles, and positions that function in the church. When God looks at His people on earth, He wants us to use our gifts for His glory and good. However, if you never use another spiritual gift. If no one ever speaks in tongues, lays hands on the sick, or prays a powerful prayer that shakes the corridors of heaven, there is still something much more important to the Lord. What is it, you ask? It is Love! Love is how our King defines Himself. The Bible says, "God is love" (1 John 4:16). Love is so important that without it, none of the gifts even matter. In this stead, Love never loses. Love always wins. Love is never defeated. Love forever overcomes. Love always endures. Love saves. Love forgives. Love shares. Love lasts forever! If you want to make God happy, learn how to love!

Day 81
"I must work the works of Him that sent me...." John 9:4

I'M NOT JUST A VOLUNTEER

A young lady recently told her friend that she volunteers at her local church. The young lady she spoke to said, "I have a church home, but I do not volunteer. I am a servant." Is there a difference between a servant and a volunteer? Yes! The word volunteer comes from the Latin word voluntare, meaning to borrow. So when you volunteer, you let people borrow your time. You let them borrow your services. However, the Greek word for servant is the term dulous. It is a reference to an enslaved person who has a Master that has been so good, kind, loving, and caring to him that the enslaved person wants to remain with this Master forever. In that light, if you are Christian and you work in your local congregation, you are not a volunteer because you have been bought with a price (1 Cor. 3:16). You are a servant that must "...work the works of Him that sent you while it is day." With this in mind, get busy if you are not serving anywhere in your church. And, if you are serving, serve like you are doing it for the Master!

Day 82
"I must work the works of Him that sent me...." John 9:4

SERVE BECAUSE I WANT TO

People serve for different reasons. Some serve to be seen. Others serve so that they can enjoy the privilege of a title being attached to their name. Yes, some still serve because they sincerely desire to give God their absolute best. Here's the truth: a servant of the Lord should serve because they want to do it. A few years ago, a church family honored a group of women for having 25 years of faithful uninterrupted service within their local congregation. It was a beautiful occasion until it became ugly. The organizing committee left one particular lady's name off the list, whose name was not on the plaque or program. The Pastor of the church contacted this wonderful lady who had over 51 years of service at the church to apologize for the oversight. To his amazement, he discovered something mind-blowing. This church matriarch was not bothered by her name not appearing on the program or the plaque. She told the Pastor that her service at the church had nothing to do with her name. It was His name that she wanted to lift. And, as long as His name was glorified, she was satisfied. She said, "I serve because I want to. I owe the Lord, and I know it."

Day 83
"I must work the works of Him that sent me...." John 9:4

SERVE BECAUSE HE HELPS ME GET THROUGH

Do you know the secret to Christian service? Do you know what it takes to keep serving and serving even when you feel like you want to quit? Are you aware of the potency of what makes a servant serve, no matter what conditions exist? Here's the secret: the prayer is that you always remember it. The secret to Christian service rests in the treasured truth that helping others helps you make it through. Sounds crazy right? But, it's the secret. You see, the more you help others, the more you help yourself. The more you open your hand to give to others, the more God gives you. The more of your life you pour out, the more the Lord of heaven pours back into you. With this in mind, service to God becomes a selfish act for the saint that serves. When Jesus says, "I must work the works of Him that sent me...." He was really speaking about the fact that His purpose on Earth was to die so that others could live. His work was the cross. The shocking news is that Jesus is not the only one with a cross. As a Christian, you have one too. Just like Jesus helps us get through life, based on His service and sacrifice, you help others you serve to do the same. If you want to make it through, help someone endure that can't help you. Helping them will help you make it through.

Day 84
"I must work the works of Him that sent me...." John 9:4

SERVE BECAUSE I GET TO

Let's face it; everybody will not let you into their private group chats. Some people won't let you into their private clubs. Some people just don't think you fit into their fraternities and sororities. You just don't cut it. But, if God had a private group, your face would be on the logo. If God had a private chat, you would be on His list to say "Good Morning,"! If God had a "fav-five" in His cell phone, your pic would be at the top. And, if God had a private counsel of selected people on the Earth that He would have hand-picked to represent worldwide, you would be in His group. With this kind of opportunity looking you in the face, you would not serve God because you had to. You would serve God by simply saying, "I Get To!" As a Christian, look at what you get to do. You get to talk to the world's creator no matter how busy He might be. You get a chance to hold His hand, even though His hands are busy governing the galaxy's affairs. You would even get a chance to call Him your Father because He has adopted you into His royal family. To serve someone like this should be something you boast about because you get to do it.

Day 85
"I must work the works of Him that sent me...." John 9:4

SERVE HIM BECAUSE HE LETS YOU

Imagine that when you rose this morning, you could not walk. And, when you tried to move your arms, they would not move one inch. Imagine that you could not chew or swallow when it was time to eat. And, when it was time for you to hear, you were deaf. Now only imagine looking towards heaven, and in the silence of your soul, you ask the Lord, "Why is this happening to me?" He responds, "I decided I wouldn't let you do it. If you're reading this devotional, God let you do it. If you can walk, talk, breathe, hear, laugh, clap, brush your teeth, wash your face, and eat breakfast, it is only because God let you do it. With this in mind, God has not only done all those things for you, the Lord has allowed you to serve Him. In this way, you should serve the Lord because He lets you do it. If you can sing, God let you sing, so sing for Him! If you can dance, God let you dance, so dance for Him! If you can greet people kindly, greet people who walk into the house of the Lord for Him. Jesus said this: "I must work the works of Him that sent me while it is day." The Apostle Paul put it like this to the Colossians "...do all in the name of the Lord Jesus..." (Col. 3:23b). Do it for God because He let you do it for Him!

Day 86
"I must work the works of Him that sent me...." John 9:4

SERVE BECAUSE HE KNOWS YOU

When Jesus says, "I must work the works of Him that sent me...." He is speaking of doing the work of His Father. In this stead, a real Father knows His Son. The story was told of a young man raised by a Father who worked hard for their family every day. His dad had three full-time jobs. Even though the family was never rich, they never missed anything because their father worked so hard. Over time, the father grew old and somewhat feeble, and the young man became an adult. When the young man looked back at the sacrifices his father had made for him, he wanted to serve him. He wanted to bless him. He wanted to do something for his father because his father knew all of his needs and met them. Though this is a story about a father and his earthly son, the truth is that this same scenario exists in the lives of every Christian and our eternal father. If you love the Lord Jesus Christ, your Heavenly Father has met your needs, and what you should do is serve Him because He knows you. He knows the doors He's opened for you. He knows the sins He's forgiven for you. And, He knows the blessings He bestowed upon you. Here's a great question for you to consider: what does God know about you that should compel you to serve Him with everything you have?

Day 87
"I must work the works of Him that sent me...." John 9:4

SERVE BECAUSE YOU NEED TO

He stood about six feet four inches tall. He had tattoos on his arms, neck, and one or two in his face. His name was Andre. Okay, let's clear the air and say Andre had been through quite a bit in his life. He had made some mistakes and taken some wrong turns. But the good news is that he made his way to church, gave the Lord his life, and was determined not to go back to what he once was but move forward into what the Lord wanted him to be. Once he had been baptized and completed New Members Orientation, he made it clear that he would serve. He was adamant about serving God and giving. They went hand in hand for this young man. When asked why he was so happy to serve, he said, "After all that I have done in my life, I'm in a space where I have to serve because I need to." You may not have tatt on your face or a rugged background littered with mistakes, but have you reached the place yet where you conclude that you should serve the Lord because you need to? If you still need to and you're not serving anywhere in the Lord's house for Him, now is the time to do it!

Day 88
"I must work the works of Him that sent me...." John 9:4

SERVE BECAUSE IT GROWS YOU

Do you ever feel that you're kinda "stuck in a rut"? If you answered yes, it could signal that you are no longer growing. Growth does not happen in a day; it happens daily. It is a process. With this in mind, growing and serving are like Siamese twins attached at the hip. And, nothing grows a believer like serving does. You will never learn to appreciate what the Lord has given you until you serve people who don't have what God has given you, and yet they still have a joy that you can't seem to buy, borrow or rent. Gladys Wyse was an eighty-eight-year-old woman stricken with a horrible muscular disorder that caused her body to be twisted like a pretzel. It was storming outside when her Pastor arrived to visit with her, and he was having a rather difficult day. He was complaining like never before. Yet, Sister Wyse was filled with joy but could not do anything for herself. Here he was standing, healthy and robust yet complaining. Then, the Pastor started realizing that it was extremely immature of him to complain when others had so much less and were still joyful and thankful. Here's the bottom line for this devotional lesson, if the Pastor grew and matured while serving, it could happen to you too. To continue serving is essentially to keep on growing. So, are you growing or just existing and feeling stuck in a rut? Be honest with your answer.

Day 89
"I must work the works of Him that sent me...." John 9:4

SERVE BECAUSE I WANT TO ENCOURAGE YOU

Jesus, from the moment of His birth, lived His life headed for the cross. Yet, while He sojourned on earth, He took the time to encourage so many people along the way. If feeding people was His only mission, He was an abysmal failure. He came to die for sure. But while heading to where He would meet His fate, He took the time to encourage others along the way. When you read the words of John 9 as our Lord encounters the blind man, born without eyes, it is clear that what Jesus wanted to do was encourage those that were wounded that He would encounter. It was a ministry of service par excellence. All born-again believers in the Lord Jesus should immolate His life and servant model. Let's do a devotional activity as our ninety-day time together slowly concludes. Find someone you may know who has been having a tough time and encourage them in the faith. Believe it or not, encouraging them will strengthen you!

Day 90
"I must work the works of Him that sent me...." John 9:4

SERVE BECAUSE I WANT TO SEE YOU

The ultimate goal of every believer on Earth should not be to make it to heaven. This is nice, but it should be something other than the goal. The real goal should be to meet God one day and hear Him say two words that signal your life's greatest accomplishment. It would simply be to hear the Lord say, "Well done." To work the works of Him that have commissioned you to service should not be to receive anything from people. It should be to have the Lord honor you through His matchless mercy and timeless grace for the good that you have tried to provide to others. He never promised that this would be easy. He never said that you would be appreciated. He said that one of these days, we will have to give an account for what has been done in our bodies in time. To see the Lord's face and to find out that He is pleased with you should be everything to you if you are a Christian. To serve like you plan to see God one day, you were graciously saved from sin because of your faith in His risen Son. And, because you knew that you owed the Lord more than you could ever repay Him, you served while you could. You helped when there was an opportunity. You worshiped every time you had a moment in the congregation of the saints. And you humbled yourself and shared His love with others through acts of Christian service that brought all of us together for God's Glory and humankind's good.

In this way, an old hymn holds within its confines the radical truth that offers blessing and eternal benefits to those who, together with others, will serve until they see Him. It says, "As I journey through the land singing as I go, Pointing souls to Calvary– to the crimson flow, Many arrows pierce my soul from without, within; but my Lord leads me on, through Him, I must win. Oh, I want to see Him, look upon His face, there to sing forever of His saving grace; On the streets of Glory let me lift my voice; cares all past, home at last, ever to rejoice."

Until this day comes for you, unite with other believers in Love for the service of our God because we are better together!

Antioch Missionary Baptist Church
3920 W. Cardinal Drive Beaumont, TX 77705
Dr. John R. Adolph, Pastor
Website www.antiochbmt.org
FaceBook: Antioch Missionary Baptist Church
IG: @antiochbmt

Worship Service
Every Sunday at 8:00 am & 10:00 am
Virtual and Personal
Website: www.antiochbmt.org
YouTube: John R. Adolph Ministries LLC.

War Room Prayer Call
Every Wednesday at 7:00 am
YouTube: John R. Adolph Ministries LLC.
Dial 667-770-1807

Bible Study
Every Thursday at 6:00 pm
Virtual and Personal
Website: www.antiochbmt.org
YouTube: John R. Adolph Ministries LLC.

John R. Adolph Ministries LLC.
The Message. The Ministry. The Man.
Website: www.jradolph.com
YouTube: John R. Adolph Ministries LLC.
FaceBook: John R. Adolph Ministries LLC.
IG: @iamjradolph

Dr. John R. Adolph

For more information contact:

Dr. John R. Adolph, Pastor
Website www.antiochbmt.org
FaceBook: Antioch Missionary Baptist Church
IG: @antiochbmt

Other Books by John R. Adolph

I'm Changing the Game: Lessons from the playbook in Paul's letter to the Philippians

Not Without A Fight: A 30-day journey of excitement

Marriage is For Losers, Celibacy is For Fools

Victory: Eternal truths that connect you with your God given destiny

I Want Some Too: A life changing look at Paul's letter to the Ephesians.

Victorious Christian Living VOL 1: A practical guide to learning Christian doctrine

To purchase additional copies of this book or other books by Dr Adolph
or visit Amazon.com or our bookstore at www.advbookstore.com

For more information on these or other titles email Advantage Books at info@advbooks.com

Orlando, Florida, USA
"we bring dreams to life"™
www.advbookstore.com

Made in United States
Orlando, FL
02 May 2024

46433450R00038